EMMANUEL JOSEPH

Recognizing the Red Flags: A Comprehensive Guide to Identifying and Escaping Abusive Relationships

Copyright © 2023 by Emmanuel Joseph

All rights reserved. No part of this publication may be reproduced, stored or transmitted in any form or by any means, electronic, mechanical, photocopying, recording, scanning, or otherwise without written permission from the publisher. It is illegal to copy this book, post it to a website, or distribute it by any other means without permission.

First edition

*This book was professionally typeset on Reedsy.
Find out more at reedsy.com*

Contents

1	Chapter 1: Introduction - Understanding Abuse and Its Impact	1
2	Chapter 2: Types of Abuse: Physical, Emotional, and...	4
3	Chapter 3: The Cycle of Abuse: Recognizing Patterns	7
4	Chapter 4: Red Flags in Dating and Early Relationships	10
5	Chapter 5: Abusive Relationships: Signs and Symptoms	13
6	Chapter 6: Gaslighting and Manipulation: How to Spot Them	16
7	Chapter 7: Codependency and Enabling: Breaking the Cycle	19
8	Chapter 8: Escaping Abusive Relationships: Planning for...	22
9	Chapter 9: Support Systems: Finding Help and Resources	25
10	Chapter 10: Healing and Recovery: Rebuilding Your Life	28
11	Chapter 11: Legal Aspects of Abusive Relationships	31
12	Chapter 12: Moving Forward: Rebuilding Your Life After Abuse	34

1

Chapter 1: Introduction - Understanding Abuse and Its Impact

Introduction

In a world where love is celebrated and cherished, it can be disheartening to acknowledge that many relationships are tainted by abuse. Abuse is a dark cloud that looms over what should be one of life's most beautiful experiences. In this book, we will embark on a journey of understanding and empowerment, exploring the complex terrain of abusive relationships, and learning how to recognize the red flags that often go unnoticed.

The Unseen Epidemic

Abusive relationships exist on a continuum, and they are alarmingly prevalent in our society. It's crucial to understand that abuse is not limited to physical violence; it can take on many forms, including emotional, psychological, and financial abuse. This chapter aims to shed light on this unseen epidemic and its far-reaching impact.

Defining Abuse

To embark on this journey, we must first define abuse. Abuse is the misuse of power and control within a relationship to harm, intimidate, or manipulate another person. It can manifest in various ways, from overt physical violence to subtle psychological manipulation. Understanding the different forms of abuse is a fundamental step toward recognizing its presence in your own life or in the lives of those you care about.

The Impact of Abuse

Abuse is not only a violation of one's physical and emotional well-being but can also erode a person's self-esteem, self-worth, and overall quality of life. Victims of abuse often endure long-lasting emotional scars that can affect their ability to form healthy relationships in the future. By recognizing the signs of abuse early, we can hope to minimize the damage it inflicts and provide a path to healing and recovery.

Breaking the Silence

One of the most challenging aspects of abusive relationships is that they often thrive in silence and isolation. Victims may feel trapped, ashamed, or fearful of speaking out. It is our collective responsibility to break the silence and create a safe space for discussing abuse openly. This book is a step in that direction, providing information and tools to empower individuals to recognize and escape abusive relationships.

In this chapter, we have introduced the concept of abuse and highlighted its various forms. We've also touched on the profound impact that abuse can have on its victims and the importance of breaking the silence surrounding it.

CHAPTER 1: INTRODUCTION - UNDERSTANDING ABUSE AND ITS IMPACT

The following chapters will delve deeper into the specifics of different types of abuse, the red flags that signal its presence, and the steps individuals can take to escape abusive relationships.

This journey is not an easy one, but it is a necessary one. By the end of this book, you will be equipped with knowledge, insight, and resources to help yourself or someone you care about navigate the difficult path to recognizing and escaping abusive relationships. Remember, the first step to empowerment is understanding, and together, we will shine a light on the darkest corners of this issue.

2

Chapter 2: Types of Abuse: Physical, Emotional, and Psychological

Understanding the many forms of abuse is essential in recognizing the red flags that can signal an abusive relationship. This chapter delves into the various types of abuse, shedding light on physical, emotional, and psychological abuse.

Physical Abuse

Physical abuse is perhaps the most visible form of abuse, as it involves the use of force to harm or intimidate another person. This can manifest in various ways, from hitting, slapping, or pushing to more severe acts of violence such as strangulation or the use of weapons. Physical abuse is often what first comes to mind when discussing abusive relationships, but it's important to understand that abuse is not limited to physical actions alone.

Emotional Abuse

Emotional abuse is a subtler, yet equally damaging, form of mistreatment. It involves tactics aimed at undermining a person's self-esteem and emotional well-being. Emotional abuse can take the form of insults, name-calling, humiliation, and constant criticism. Abusers often use manipulation to control their victims, causing them to doubt their worth and sanity. This form of abuse can be incredibly insidious, as the wounds it inflicts are often invisible.

Psychological Abuse

Psychological abuse delves even deeper into the realm of manipulation and control. It includes gaslighting, a tactic used to make the victim doubt their perception of reality. Abusers may employ mind games, isolation, and threats to maintain power over their victims. This form of abuse can leave lasting scars on a person's psyche, making it difficult to trust one's own judgment and escape the relationship.

The Intersection of Abuse Types

It's important to recognize that these forms of abuse often intersect. Physical abuse is frequently accompanied by emotional and psychological abuse. In some cases, emotional and psychological abuse can be as damaging, if not more so, than physical violence. Understanding these nuances is crucial to recognizing red flags in abusive relationships.

Recognizing the Signs

In this chapter, we've explored the different types of abuse, from the visible physical abuse to the more subtle emotional and psychological tactics. The key to recognizing the signs of abuse is to understand that it can take on multiple forms. By being aware of the various ways abuse can manifest, you are better equipped to identify red flags in your own relationship or those of people you care about.

In the chapters to come, we will delve deeper into the specific red flags associated with each type of abuse, as well as strategies for responding to these signs and seeking help. Recognizing the red flags is the first step on the path to escaping an abusive relationship and rebuilding a life free from the shadow of abuse.

3

Chapter 3: The Cycle of Abuse: Recognizing Patterns

Introduction

Abuse in relationships often follows a recurring pattern, a cycle that can be difficult to escape without a clear understanding of its stages. In this chapter, we will delve into the cycle of abuse, helping you recognize the common patterns that many abusive relationships follow. Understanding this cycle is a vital step in breaking free from its grip.

The Cycle of Abuse

The cycle of abuse typically consists of three main phases: the tension-building phase, the acute abuse phase, and the honeymoon phase. Recognizing these phases can provide insight into the dynamics of an abusive relationship.

1. Tension-Building Phase

This phase is marked by growing tension, arguments, and conflicts between the partners. Communication breaks down, and minor disputes escalate. The victim often feels like they are walking on eggshells, trying to avoid triggering the abuser's anger. This phase creates a sense of impending doom and fear.

2. Acute Abuse Phase

The tension in the previous phase reaches its breaking point, leading to an outburst of abusive behavior. This can involve physical violence, emotional abuse, or psychological manipulation. It's during this phase that the victim experiences the most harm and fear.

3. Honeymoon Phase

After the acute abuse phase, the abuser often becomes remorseful and apologetic. They may shower the victim with affection, promises to change, and gifts. This phase can be confusing, as the victim may believe that the abuser has genuinely changed. However, it is often a temporary respite before the cycle begins again.

Breaking the Cycle

Recognizing the cycle of abuse is a crucial step in identifying an abusive relationship. However, it is not always easy to break free from this pattern, as victims often hold onto hope during the honeymoon phase. It's important to understand that the cycle can repeat indefinitely unless decisive action is taken.

Empowerment and Support

Breaking free from the cycle of abuse requires support and empowerment. Victims often face numerous barriers, such as fear, financial dependence, or emotional attachment. In the chapters to come, we will explore strategies for escaping abusive relationships and finding the support necessary to begin

CHAPTER 3: THE CYCLE OF ABUSE: RECOGNIZING PATTERNS

the journey toward healing and recovery.

Conclusion

In this chapter, we've discussed the cycle of abuse, a recurring pattern that many abusive relationships follow. Recognizing the tension-building phase, acute abuse phase, and honeymoon phase can be instrumental in identifying an abusive relationship. However, the process of breaking free from this cycle is challenging and complex, and it will be the focus of subsequent chapters.

Understanding the cycle of abuse is the first step to breaking its hold on your life or the life of someone you care about. By recognizing these patterns, you can begin the journey toward a future free from the cycle of abuse and filled with healthier, more fulfilling relationships.

4

Chapter 4: Red Flags in Dating and Early Relationships

Introduction

The early stages of a relationship are a time of excitement and discovery, but they can also be a critical period for recognizing red flags that might signal the potential for abuse. In this chapter, we will explore the warning signs that can emerge during dating and the initial phases of a relationship, helping you make informed decisions to protect your well-being.

Red Flags in Dating

1. Isolation from Friends and Family

One of the earliest red flags in an abusive relationship is when your partner attempts to isolate you from your friends and family. They might discourage you from spending time with loved ones, making you feel more dependent on them for emotional support.

2. Excessive Jealousy and Possessiveness

CHAPTER 4: RED FLAGS IN DATING AND EARLY RELATIONSHIPS

Unhealthy jealousy and possessiveness can be a sign of controlling behavior. If your partner constantly questions your actions, friendships, or whereabouts, it's essential to recognize this as a potential red flag.

3. Verbal or Emotional Aggression

Even in the early stages of a relationship, pay attention to how your partner communicates. If they engage in name-calling, insults, or frequent emotional outbursts, it's a concerning sign.

4. Pressure for Rapid Commitment

An abusive partner might rush the relationship, pressuring you into making major commitments before you're ready. This can include moving in together, getting married, or having children.

5. Withholding Affection or Love

If your partner withholds affection, love, or intimacy as a form of control, it's a clear red flag. In healthy relationships, emotional and physical intimacy should be mutual and freely given.

Red Flags in Early Relationships

1. Chronic Unpredictability

In the early stages of a relationship, unpredictability can be thrilling, but chronic unpredictability is a sign of instability. If your partner's moods or behaviors drastically fluctuate, it can indicate future issues.

2. Boundary Violations

Healthy relationships respect boundaries. If your partner consistently disregards your boundaries, whether physical, emotional, or personal, it's an alarming sign.

3. History of Abuse

Be cautious if your partner has a history of abusive behavior in previous relationships. While people can change, it's essential to approach such situations with caution and awareness.

4. Manipulation and Gaslighting

Gaslighting, which involves manipulating your perception of reality, can begin in the early stages of a relationship. If you find yourself constantly doubting your own judgment, it's a significant red flag.

Conclusion

Recognizing red flags in dating and early relationships is a crucial skill for preventing abusive relationships from taking hold. It's essential to trust your instincts and not ignore signs of controlling or abusive behavior. In the following chapters, we will explore strategies for responding to these red flags and making informed decisions about the future of the relationship.

Remember that the early stages of a relationship are a time for getting to know each other, not for sacrificing your well-being and independence. By being vigilant and informed, you can make choices that promote healthy, respectful relationships and avoid falling into the trap of an abusive one.

5

Chapter 5: Abusive Relationships: Signs and Symptoms

Introduction

As relationships progress, the signs of abuse can become more apparent, and the impact on the victim's well-being can intensify. In this chapter, we will explore the signs and symptoms of abusive relationships, providing you with a deeper understanding of what to look for if you suspect you or someone you care about is in such a relationship.

Recognizing Signs of Abuse

1. Physical Signs

Physical signs of abuse may include unexplained injuries, frequent visits to the hospital, or a partner who avoids discussing these injuries or offers inconsistent explanations for them.

2. Emotional and Psychological Distress

Victims of abuse often experience emotional and psychological distress. Symptoms can range from chronic anxiety, depression, and low self-esteem to unexplained mood swings and emotional instability.

3. Social Isolation

Abusers may intentionally isolate their partners from friends and family. If you or someone you know suddenly becomes more withdrawn or disengaged from social activities, it may be a sign of isolation, a tactic used in abusive relationships.

4. Control Over Finances

Abusers often exert control over their victims' finances. Signs of financial abuse include restricted access to money, being forced to justify expenses, or feeling financially dependent on the abuser.

5. Constant Fear and Anxiety

Living in fear is a common experience in an abusive relationship. Victims may exhibit signs of constant anxiety, hypervigilance, or a fear of the partner's reactions.

6. Sexual Abuse and Coercion

In abusive relationships, sexual abuse can be prevalent. Victims may display signs of discomfort or distress related to sexual intimacy. Coercion and non-consensual activities are also common in such cases.

7. Attempts to Hide or Excuse Behavior

Victims often try to hide or excuse their partner's abusive behavior. This might manifest as evading questions about injuries, denying that the abuse is

CHAPTER 5: ABUSIVE RELATIONSHIPS: SIGNS AND SYMPTOMS

happening, or blaming themselves for the partner's actions.

8. Changes in Behavior and Personality

Abusive relationships can lead to significant changes in a person's behavior and personality. You may notice a once-confident and outgoing individual become introverted, anxious, or withdrawn.

Responding to Signs of Abuse

Recognizing the signs and symptoms of abuse is a critical first step. Responding to these signs often involves providing support and assistance to the victim. In the following chapters, we will discuss strategies for helping those in abusive relationships and how to plan for safety and escape when necessary.

It's essential to remember that abuse is never the fault of the victim, and it's never too late to seek help or support. This chapter equips you with the knowledge to identify the signs of an abusive relationship, allowing you to take action to protect yourself or someone you care about from further harm.

6

Chapter 6: Gaslighting and Manipulation: How to Spot Them

Introduction

Gaslighting and manipulation are insidious tactics used by abusers to maintain control and power in relationships. In this chapter, we will explore what gaslighting and manipulation entail and provide you with the tools to recognize and respond to these harmful behaviors.

Understanding Gaslighting

Gaslighting is a form of psychological manipulation in which an abuser attempts to make their victim doubt their perception, memory, or sanity. This tactic is used to create confusion and dependency on the abuser. Recognizing gaslighting can be challenging, as it often occurs gradually and subtly.

Signs of Gaslighting

1. Denial and Minimization: The abuser denies their actions or minimizes their impact, making the victim feel as though they are exaggerating or

CHAPTER 6: GASLIGHTING AND MANIPULATION: HOW TO SPOT THEM

imagining things.

2. Projection: The abuser accuses the victim of the very behavior they are engaging in. This can lead the victim to question their own actions and motives.

3. Invalidation: The abuser invalidates the victim's emotions or experiences, telling them they are "too sensitive" or "crazy" for feeling the way they do.

4. Withholding Information: The abuser withholds information, leaving the victim in the dark and unable to make informed decisions.

5. Shifting Blame: The abuser shifts blame onto the victim, making them feel responsible for the abuser's actions.

Recognizing Manipulation

Manipulation is the use of tactics to control or influence another person's thoughts, feelings, or actions to the manipulator's advantage. It often goes hand-in-hand with gaslighting in abusive relationships. Recognizing manipulation is crucial in identifying an abusive dynamic.

Signs of Manipulation

1. Guilt Tripping: The manipulator uses guilt to get their way, making the victim feel responsible for the manipulator's happiness or well-being.

2. Love-Bombing: In the early stages of a relationship, the manipulator showers the victim with affection and attention but withdraws it when they don't get what they want.

3. Threats and Ultimatums: Manipulators may use threats or ultimatums to gain compliance or control over their partner.

4. Silent Treatment: The manipulator may use the silent treatment as a way to punish the victim and force them into submission.

5. Playing the Victim: Manipulators often play the victim to gain sympathy and manipulate others into taking their side.

Responding to Gaslighting and Manipulation

Responding to gaslighting and manipulation can be challenging but is essential for protecting your emotional well-being. It often involves setting boundaries, seeking support, and even considering the possibility of leaving the relationship.

In the following chapters, we will explore strategies for responding to these tactics, planning for safety, and seeking help when needed. Understanding and identifying gaslighting and manipulation are key steps toward reclaiming your independence and emotional health.

Conclusion

Gaslighting and manipulation are tactics used by abusers to control and manipulate their victims. Recognizing these behaviors can be difficult, but it's a crucial step in identifying an abusive relationship. In the chapters to come, we will delve deeper into strategies for responding to gaslighting, manipulation, and the broader issue of abuse. Remember that seeking help and support is a sign of strength, and there are resources available to assist you in navigating these challenging situations.

7

Chapter 7: Codependency and Enabling: Breaking the Cycle

Introduction

In many abusive relationships, a complex dynamic of codependency and enabling can take hold, perpetuating the cycle of abuse. In this chapter, we will explore the concept of codependency, enabling, and how to break free from these patterns to regain personal autonomy and well-being.

Understanding Codependency

Codependency is a dysfunctional and one-sided relationship pattern in which one person's emotional and psychological needs are consistently put aside in favor of the other's. This pattern can arise in abusive relationships, where the victim becomes emotionally enmeshed with the abuser, often to their detriment.

Signs of Codependency

1. Excessive Caretaking: The codependent individual often takes on the role

of caretaker, sacrificing their own needs and desires to meet the needs of the abusive partner.

2. Low Self-Esteem: Codependent individuals typically have low self-esteem and may seek validation and self-worth through their relationship with the abuser.

3. Fear of Abandonment: The codependent person fears abandonment and is willing to endure mistreatment to avoid being alone.

4. Difficulty Setting Boundaries: Codependents have difficulty setting healthy boundaries and often tolerate unacceptable behavior from their partners.

5. Denial of the Problem: Codependents often deny the severity of the abuse or the need to leave the relationship, believing they can "fix" the abuser.

Understanding Enabling

Enabling is a behavior that allows an abuser to continue their harmful actions by shielding them from the consequences. It often goes hand-in-hand with codependency, as the codependent partner may enable the abusive behavior to maintain the relationship.

Signs of Enabling

1. Making Excuses: Enablers often make excuses for the abusive partner's actions, rationalizing or justifying their behavior.

2. Taking Responsibility for the Abuser's Actions: Enablers may assume responsibility for the consequences of the abuser's actions, such as covering up their mistakes or taking the blame.

3. Rescuing the Abuser: Enablers may continually rescue the abusive partner

CHAPTER 7: CODEPENDENCY AND ENABLING: BREAKING THE CYCLE

from the negative outcomes of their actions, preventing them from facing the consequences of their behavior.

Breaking the Cycle

Breaking free from the cycle of codependency and enabling is challenging but necessary for personal growth and escaping an abusive relationship.

1. Recognize and Acknowledge Codependency: The first step is recognizing and acknowledging your codependent patterns. This self-awareness is crucial for initiating change.

2. Seek Support: Reach out to support networks, such as friends, family, or support groups. These connections can provide emotional support and encouragement.

3. Set Boundaries: Learn to establish and maintain healthy boundaries, ensuring your emotional and psychological well-being is a priority.

4. Therapy and Counseling: Consider therapy or counseling to address codependent tendencies, heal emotional wounds, and build a stronger sense of self.

Conclusion

Codependency and enabling often reinforce the cycle of abuse, making it challenging to escape. Recognizing these patterns and taking steps to break free from them are essential for regaining personal autonomy and well-being.

In the upcoming chapters, we will continue to explore strategies for healing and recovery, as well as ways to rebuild your life after escaping an abusive relationship. Remember that seeking help and making changes in your life are powerful steps toward a brighter, healthier future.

8

Chapter 8: Escaping Abusive Relationships: Planning for Safety

Introduction

Escaping an abusive relationship is a daunting and crucial step for anyone who finds themselves trapped in such a situation. In this chapter, we will explore the essential aspects of planning for safety when leaving an abusive relationship.

Assessing Your Situation

Before taking action to leave an abusive relationship, it's crucial to assess your specific situation and safety risks. Factors to consider include:

1. Severity of Abuse: Evaluate the severity of the abuse and any imminent physical threats.

2. Resources and Support: Identify your support system, such as friends, family, or organizations that can assist you.

3. Financial Independence: Assess your financial situation and the potential need for financial resources when leaving.

4. Legal Considerations: Understand legal aspects, such as restraining orders or child custody, that may apply to your situation.

Creating a Safety Plan

A safety plan is a personalized, step-by-step guide for leaving an abusive relationship safely. While each plan will be unique to the individual's circumstances, a basic safety plan typically includes the following components:

1. Emergency Contacts: List trusted friends, family, and local domestic violence hotlines that you can contact during an emergency.

2. Safe Locations: Identify safe places you can go to when you need to leave your current environment, such as a friend's house, a domestic violence shelter, or a public space.

3. Financial Resources: Ensure access to money or financial resources that will allow you to support yourself when you leave.

4. Legal Measures: Understand and consider legal measures such as restraining orders or child custody arrangements to protect your rights.

5. Documentation: Secure important documents, including identification, passports, birth certificates, and legal documents, in a safe and accessible place.

6. Safety Signals: Develop a system of signals with friends or family to indicate that you need help discreetly.

7. Packing Essentials: Prepare a bag with essential items, including clothing,

medications, and personal items, to take with you when you leave.

8. Children and Pets: Consider the safety of any children or pets in your care and plan for their protection.

Seeking Professional Assistance

Leaving an abusive relationship often necessitates professional help. Reach out to local domestic violence shelters, organizations, or support groups to access resources and guidance. These organizations can provide not only shelter but also legal and emotional support.

The process of leaving an abusive relationship is complex and fraught with challenges. It's essential to remember that you don't have to go through it alone. Support networks and professional assistance are invaluable resources in planning your escape to safety.

Conclusion

Planning for safety is a crucial step in leaving an abusive relationship. Safety plans are tailored to your unique circumstances, ensuring that you have the resources and support needed to escape harm and rebuild your life. In the upcoming chapters, we will continue to explore strategies for healing, recovery, and rebuilding your life after escaping an abusive relationship. Remember that you deserve to live a life free from abuse and filled with safety and happiness.

9

Chapter 9: Support Systems: Finding Help and Resources

Introduction

Escaping an abusive relationship is a challenging journey that becomes significantly more manageable with the right support systems in place. In this chapter, we will explore the crucial role of support systems and the resources available to help individuals break free from abusive relationships.

The Power of Support

Support systems are an essential lifeline for those seeking to escape an abusive relationship. They provide emotional, practical, and sometimes financial assistance, as well as a sense of security during a difficult time.

1. Friends and Family: Your loved ones can be a primary source of support. Trusted friends and family members can offer a safe place to stay, emotional encouragement, and assistance with practical matters.

2. Support Groups: Joining a support group for survivors of abuse can

provide a sense of community and understanding. These groups offer a space to share experiences, advice, and resources.

3. Counseling and Therapy: Professional therapists and counselors can offer individual and group therapy to help survivors heal from the emotional scars of abuse.

4. Domestic Violence Shelters: Domestic violence shelters provide safe accommodation and support for those fleeing abusive relationships. They can offer refuge, resources, and counseling.

5. Legal Assistance: Legal aid organizations and pro bono lawyers can provide guidance on legal matters such as restraining orders, child custody, and divorce proceedings.

6. Hotlines and Helplines: Domestic violence hotlines and helplines offer immediate assistance, information, and referrals to resources for individuals in crisis.

Resources for Healing and Recovery

In addition to emotional support, various resources are available to help survivors of abuse heal and rebuild their lives.

1. Safety Plans: Continually update your safety plan to ensure you have the necessary resources and contacts in case of emergencies.

2. Counseling Services: Seek therapy and counseling services to address the emotional impact of abuse and develop strategies for healing and personal growth.

3. Legal Aid: Consult with legal professionals to understand your rights, secure restraining orders, and establish custody arrangements if necessary.

CHAPTER 9: SUPPORT SYSTEMS: FINDING HELP AND RESOURCES

4. Financial Resources: Access financial support, if available, to help cover living expenses and establish financial independence.

5. Housing Assistance: Investigate housing programs that provide safe and affordable accommodations for survivors.

6. Employment Services: Employment assistance programs can aid survivors in securing stable employment, supporting their financial independence.

7. Educational Resources: Explore opportunities for education and skill development to enhance your long-term prospects.

It's important to reach out to these resources and take advantage of the help and guidance they offer. Remember that seeking support is a sign of strength and resilience.

Conclusion

Support systems and resources are essential in the process of escaping an abusive relationship and rebuilding one's life. In the upcoming chapters, we will continue to explore strategies for healing, recovery, and personal growth after leaving an abusive relationship. You don't have to face this journey alone; there are people and organizations ready to provide assistance and help you take the steps toward a safer and brighter future.

10

Chapter 10: Healing and Recovery: Rebuilding Your Life

Introduction

Escaping an abusive relationship is a significant achievement, but the journey to healing and recovery is equally important. In this chapter, we will explore the process of rebuilding your life after leaving an abusive relationship, focusing on self-care, emotional well-being, and personal growth.

Reclaiming Your Independence

Leaving an abusive relationship is the first step in reclaiming your independence. To rebuild your life, it's crucial to:

1. Establish Boundaries: Learn to set and maintain healthy boundaries to protect your emotional well-being.

2. Financial Independence: Work on financial independence, including finding stable employment and managing your finances.

CHAPTER 10: HEALING AND RECOVERY: REBUILDING YOUR LIFE

3. Safety and Security: Create a safe and secure living environment where you have control over your personal space and well-being.

4. Legal Support: Address any legal matters related to child custody, restraining orders, or divorce proceedings to protect your rights.

5. Healthy Relationships: Be mindful of forming new relationships and ensure they are based on mutual respect and trust.

Emotional Healing

Emotional healing is a vital component of recovery after an abusive relationship. Here are some steps to support your emotional well-being:

1. Therapy and Counseling: Continue therapy and counseling to address the emotional scars of abuse and develop strategies for healing.

2. Self-Care: Prioritize self-care by focusing on your physical and mental health. This includes exercise, a balanced diet, and regular relaxation and stress-management techniques.

3. Journaling: Consider keeping a journal to process your emotions and thoughts as part of your healing journey.

4. Support Systems: Lean on your support systems, including friends, family, and support groups, for emotional encouragement.

5. Forgiveness and Acceptance: Work toward forgiveness and acceptance of your past while understanding that healing is a process.

Personal Growth

Recovery from an abusive relationship offers an opportunity for personal growth and transformation:

1. Education and Skill Development: Pursue opportunities for education and skill development to enhance your career prospects.

2. Setting Goals: Establish goals and a vision for your future, allowing yourself to dream and aim for a brighter tomorrow.

3. Self-Discovery: Embrace self-discovery as you learn about your strengths, values, and what truly matters to you.

4. Empowerment: Take back control of your life and embrace your newfound independence and self-empowerment.

5. Advocacy and Awareness: Consider getting involved in advocacy and raising awareness about abuse and its impact on individuals and communities.

Conclusion

Rebuilding your life after an abusive relationship is a transformative journey filled with challenges and triumphs. By prioritizing self-care, healing, and personal growth, you can emerge from the shadows of abuse as a stronger, more resilient individual.

In the upcoming chapters, we will continue to explore strategies for healing and self-empowerment, ensuring that you have the tools and knowledge needed to create a future that is free from the shadow of abuse and filled with the promise of a better life. Remember, you are not defined by your past, but rather by your courage and strength in overcoming it.

11

Chapter 11: Legal Aspects of Abusive Relationships

Introduction

Understanding the legal aspects of abusive relationships is essential for ensuring your rights and safety. In this chapter, we will explore the legal dimensions of abusive relationships, including restraining orders, child custody, and the role of law enforcement.

Legal Protection

The legal system can provide essential protection for those leaving abusive relationships. Key legal aspects to consider include:

1. Restraining Orders: Restraining orders, also known as protection orders or orders of protection, are legal documents that prevent an abusive partner from contacting or approaching you. Understanding the process of obtaining and enforcing restraining orders is crucial for your safety.

2. Child Custody: If children are involved, understanding your rights and

responsibilities in child custody matters is vital. Legal support is often necessary to navigate the complexities of custody arrangements.

3. Divorce Proceedings: If married, the legal process of divorce may be required. Consult with legal professionals to ensure a fair and equitable dissolution of your marriage.

4. Property and Asset Division: In some cases, dividing shared assets and property may be a part of the legal process. Understanding the laws regarding property division is essential.

5. Criminal Charges: In cases of severe abuse, the abuser may face criminal charges. Collaborating with law enforcement and legal professionals can help ensure a fair and just legal process.

Working with Legal Professionals

Engaging with legal professionals is often essential when navigating the legal aspects of abusive relationships:

1. Seek Legal Counsel: Consult with an attorney who specializes in family law, domestic violence, or other relevant areas. They can provide advice, representation, and assistance in legal proceedings.

2. Document Abuse: Maintain records and documentation of abusive incidents, injuries, threats, and any communication with the abusive partner. This documentation can be crucial in legal matters.

3. Testify in Court: Be prepared to testify in court if required, providing evidence and testimony to support your case.

4. Safety During Legal Proceedings: Discuss safety measures with your legal counsel, such as precautions to take during court appearances or legal

CHAPTER 11: LEGAL ASPECTS OF ABUSIVE RELATIONSHIPS

proceedings.

Legal Assistance and Resources

Accessing legal assistance and resources is essential for navigating the legal aspects of abusive relationships:

1. Legal Aid Organizations: Seek out legal aid organizations that provide free or low-cost legal assistance to those in need.

2. Crisis Intervention Services: Crisis intervention organizations may offer legal advocacy services to assist in obtaining restraining orders and navigating legal processes.

3. Domestic Violence Support Centers: Domestic violence support centers often provide legal resources and guidance for survivors.

4. Law Enforcement: Collaborate with law enforcement to report abuse and ensure your safety. They can provide information on pressing charges and obtaining protective orders.

5. Shelters and Support Groups: Shelters and support groups can connect you with legal advocates who specialize in domestic violence cases.

Conclusion

Understanding the legal aspects of abusive relationships is crucial for protecting your rights and ensuring your safety. The legal system offers important resources and protection for survivors of abuse. In the final chapter of this book, we will reflect on the journey you've embarked on and provide insights on moving forward to build healthy, fulfilling relationships and a life free from abuse. Remember that you have the right to live without fear and with the support of the law to protect your well-being.

12

Chapter 12: Moving Forward: Rebuilding Your Life After Abuse

Introduction

Leaving an abusive relationship is a momentous achievement, but it is only the beginning of your journey toward a brighter, healthier future. In this final chapter, we will explore the essential steps for moving forward, healing, and rebuilding your life after abuse.

The Journey of Recovery

Recovery from an abusive relationship is a transformative journey that involves several crucial components:

1. Self-Reflection: Take time for self-reflection to understand your experiences, emotions, and the impact of the abuse on your life.

2. Emotional Healing: Continue the process of emotional healing through therapy, counseling, and self-care. Recognize that healing takes time and effort.

CHAPTER 12: MOVING FORWARD: REBUILDING YOUR LIFE AFTER ABUSE

3. Personal Growth: Embrace personal growth and self-discovery as you define your values, interests, and goals for the future.

4. Healthy Relationships: Focus on cultivating healthy relationships based on trust, respect, and mutual support.

5. Empowerment: Embrace your newfound independence and self-empowerment as you take control of your life.

6. Advocacy: Consider getting involved in advocacy and raising awareness about abuse to support others in their healing journeys.

Rebuilding Your Life

Rebuilding your life after abuse involves several practical and emotional aspects:

1. Financial Independence: Continue working toward financial independence through stable employment, budgeting, and financial planning.

2. Legal Matters: Address any ongoing legal matters, such as child custody, restraining orders, and property division.

3. Housing and Safety: Ensure you have a safe and secure living environment where your safety and well-being are paramount.

4. Self-Care: Prioritize self-care and maintain a healthy lifestyle through regular exercise, a balanced diet, and stress-management techniques.

5. Support Systems: Lean on your support systems, including friends, family, support groups, and therapy, to provide emotional encouragement.

6. Long-Term Goals: Set long-term goals and a vision for your future,

allowing yourself to dream and aim for a brighter tomorrow.

Moving Forward with Confidence

Moving forward with confidence requires patience, resilience, and self-compassion. Here are some key principles to keep in mind:

1. Self-Compassion: Be kind and patient with yourself. Healing takes time, and you may experience setbacks along the way. This is a normal part of the healing process.

2. Seeking Help: Don't hesitate to seek help and support from professionals and support networks whenever needed. You don't have to go through this journey alone.

3. Forgiveness: Work toward forgiveness, but remember that forgiving does not mean forgetting. It is about freeing yourself from the burden of anger and resentment.

4. Learning from the Past: Use your experiences as a source of wisdom and strength. You have the capacity to emerge from adversity as a more resilient and empowered individual.

Conclusion

Leaving an abusive relationship is a monumental step toward a brighter future, but the journey doesn't end there. Your path to healing, personal growth, and rebuilding your life is a testament to your courage and resilience.

In the pages of this book, we've explored the red flags of abusive relationships, the cycle of abuse, and the various forms of support and resources available to survivors. By recognizing the signs and seeking help, you've embarked on a journey of transformation and recovery.

CHAPTER 12: MOVING FORWARD: REBUILDING YOUR LIFE AFTER ABUSE

Moving forward, remember that you are not defined by your past but by the strength and resilience that brought you to this point. Your future is filled with the potential for healthy, fulfilling relationships and a life free from the shadows of abuse. You deserve happiness, safety, and the opportunity to thrive.

www.ingramcontent.com/pod-product-compliance
Lightning Source LLC
Chambersburg PA
CBHW070442010526
44118CB00014B/2162